Trau[illegible]

Building a Trauma-informed Worshipping Community

Joanna Naomi Douglas

GROVE BOOKS LIMITED
RIDLEY HALL RD CAMBRIDGE CB3 9HU

Contents

1 Introduction 3

2 What is Trauma? 5

3 Theology and Trauma 11

4 The Witnessing of Trauma 15

5 Building a Trauma-informed Worshipping Community 19

Notes 25

Acknowledgments

My deepest acknowledgments go to all those who have walked alongside me in my journey of restoration, who have witnessed my trauma, shown me the compassion of Jesus and who believed in me when I could not believe in myself.

First Impression September 2023

ISSN 0144-171X

ISBN 978 1 78827 341 1

Introduction

1

Suffering and trauma are not new. They have existed throughout time and are a fundamental part of the human experience. The fall of Adam and Eve brought suffering and trauma into the world alongside decay and death. Ever since, humanity has been grappling with the twin needs to find a way to survive and to overcome pain. Throughout the biblical narratives, suffering and trauma remain central themes. In the Old Testament for example, Job cried out to God in a time of great personal anguish (Job 30.20–30), Tamar was raped by her brother (2 Sam 13.1–22), and many psalms lament with the burden of suffering. Our Christian faith itself stands firmly rooted in a central event of horrific trauma within the passion of Christ. Christ himself professes that his torturous suffering and death is the will of God to which he agrees, surrendering himself as a willing sacrifice (Luke 22.42). This, alongside the many narratives of trauma endured by humanity, forces Christianity to continue to grapple with the challenge of suffering and trauma and the will of a good God, something people of faith have been grappling with throughout our history.

Even now, Christianity does not offer a simple theological or pastoral response to give to the trauma survivor who has faced what can seem to be insurmountable suffering. It is easy for us to know that God is good when life is also good, but when life is hard—when it is not what we have dreamed it would be and when sins are committed against us that break us—it becomes similarly hard to know the goodness of God. Some Christians try to shy away from issues of trauma, pain and suffering as they force us to question and reframe what we know of the world, of our communities, of our individual selves, and, often most devastatingly, of God. It is difficult to sit comfortably with and alongside the trauma survivor who is contemporaneously living with trauma, because to live with trauma is to challenge the very meaning of the cross, bringing into question the death and resurrection of Jesus. The reality that a believer who is saved and redeemed by Christ is still condemned to live with trauma is often difficult to comprehend. However, individuals amid these painful suffering experiences are turning to our worshipping communities for answers to their pain; therefore it is imperative that our worshipping communities begin to understand the difficulties of trauma to support adequately and respond to survivors' needs. Isaiah said of Jesus that he is anointed to proclaim good news to the poor, sent to bind

To live with trauma is to challenge the very meaning of the cross

up the brokenhearted, 'to proclaim freedom for the captives and release from darkness for the prisoners…to comfort all who mourn, and provide for those who grieve in Zion—to bestow on them a crown of beauty instead of ashes, the oil of joy instead of mourning, and a garment of praise instead of a spirit of despair' (Isa 61.1–3). As Christians, we are called to be like Jesus in the way that we respond to those who live with the brokenness of the world, and so this too is our mandate.

Over the past few decades, there has been an ever-increasing drive towards acknowledging issues of mental health, as well as fostering a greater acceptance and understanding for those who live with mental ill-health. However, there is a clear psychological distinction between clinical mental ill-health, such as depression and anxiety, and trauma-related mental ill-health, a distinction which has not always been understood. Unfortunately, this can lead to greater stigmatization and a lack of understanding of those living with more complex trauma-related issues. Although the manifesting symptoms and behaviours may often appear similar, the root causes of clinical mental ill-health are significantly different from those of trauma-related mental ill-health and therefore should be treated and responded to differently. Clinical-related mental illnesses are caused by chemical imbalances within the brain and can largely be treated with some form of talking therapy, such as counselling, and cognitive behavioural therapy (CBT), and medication when needed. However, trauma-related mental ill-health is caused by a psychological wounding to the brain which has devastating, lifelong consequences for the survivor. This psychological trauma wounding takes the survivor beyond the capabilities of talking therapies, and a much deeper understanding of recovery processes is then required by those pastorally caring for trauma survivors.

Trauma wounding takes the survivor beyond the capabilities of talking therapies

This booklet seeks to provide an understanding of trauma-related mental ill-health and how and why it occurs by first providing a deeper understanding of the biology of the human brain and how trauma experiences impact the survivor's psychological processing. By understanding this, our worshipping communities may be better equipped to build welcoming, inclusive and trauma-informed spaces, becoming safer, more loving and supportive environments for those living with the wounding of trauma. Through these trauma-informed worshipping communities we will see psychological trauma survivors finding freedom, truly being comforted in their mourning and experiencing their brokenness being bound up in a way that allows them to access and experience the healing of Jesus.

2

What is Trauma?

The word trauma is derived from a Greek root which means a wound, tear or rupture.[1] Trauma can be applied to any experience of pain, suffering, and distress which has wounded a survivor physically and / or psychologically. For a long time, this term was associated with solely physical wounds. However, more recently it is recognized that trauma can also be a psychological wounding with methods of study into various forms of psychological trauma being developed. These began with the studies of shell shock after the First World War. This later led to the post-traumatic stress disorder (PTSD) diagnosis which was developed in the USA in the care of veterans of the Vietnam War. Later studies of similar trauma symptoms in cases of domestic and sexual abuse led to a wider understanding of psychological trauma and its symptoms. However, trauma research still does not have a clear, accepted, singular definition of psychological trauma due to the complexities and variables found within psychological trauma wounding. However, in attempting such a definition Jennifer Beste describes psychological trauma as 'the experience of terror, loss of control, and utter helplessness during a stressful event that threatens one's...psychological integrity.'[2] It is this which causes a wounding in the brain that occurs subconsciously as a way for the person to cope with, survive and endure experiences which are by their nature too painful to simply overcome.

While every person has experienced suffering, not every person has experienced trauma

Since the fall in Genesis, it is a natural part of human existence to experience some level of pain and suffering that has caused emotional distress and challenges one's perception of goodness and safety in the world. But while every person has experienced, and will experience, suffering, not every person has experienced trauma. The difference lies in their causal, but not always correlating, relationship; suffering is the experience of pain, difficulty, challenges and hardship, and sometimes causes trauma if the experience is serious enough to result in a psychological wounding that affects the brain's response to the event or events. Trauma theologian Shelley Rambo describes this relationship between the suffering experience and the trauma wounding aptly when she states that 'trauma is suffering that remains.'[3]

The Brain's Response to Suffering

The human brain is designed for survival, and at its most fundamental level is constantly trying to be prepared for any eventuality. Its basic structure is divided into many distinct complementary but separate parts, each with its function and purpose. There are three main segments which are used for feeling, processing, understanding and storing the memory of our experiences. Together these three parts are called the tripartite brain and are:

- *The reptilian brain*, which is at the base of the skull and is the part of the brain which is fully functioning at birth. It regulates primitive bodily functions such as sleep, breathing, bowel and bladder control, the feeling of pain and hunger, as well as developing habitual behaviours.
- *The limbic system* (commonly known as the emotional brain), is a part of the brain which begins to develop at a rapid pace around the age of two years old. It regulates behaviour and moves us away from acting purely on instinct as babies do. It is made up of *the thalamus, the amygdala, the hippocampus and the hypothalamus.* These assess all new and incoming information and experiences more globally by feeling, regulating, understanding and framing the emotions present during daily experiences. It is the part of the brain which builds relationships, supports understanding and coping within social structures and develops affection for others. The limbic system is also the part of the brain which facilitates memory storage and retrieval. It also feels the sights, sounds, smells, emotions and physical sensations of all our experiences, including suffering experiences, and determines if these experiences are safe or not.
- *The pre-frontal cortex* is the rational, cognitive part of the brain which regulates our understanding of our experiences and the world around us. It does this by rationally processing them and giving them meaning. It is the part of the brain which helps us understand how the world and the people within it work. It also allows us to understand our own individual identities and regulate our varied relationships. It also helps us plan what we will do in our day and gives us structure and helps us plan how to drive towards our dreams and aspirations. This is the part of the brain which deals with intellect, language, vocabulary, and all forms of communication.[4]

The limbic system forms the God-given survival mechanism. All imputing sensory information—everything we experience, sights, sounds, smells, emotions etc—is first registered and *felt* by the limbic system, specifically the thalamus. The thalamus then processes the inputting experience by sending it to the amygdala, known as the fear centre. The amygdala works alongside the hippocampus which is associated with memory and learning from past experiences. Together they determine if the sensory experience is safe or not, then process the experience in one of two ways. Our normal sensory experiences when we are not in imminent danger are processed through the amygdala and onto the pre-frontal cortex. This allows the experience to be felt by the emotional brain, and then to be regulated and given meaning, rational, cognitive thought, language and vocabulary by the pre-frontal cortex, and then is able to be stored in the long-term memory.

However, if the amygdala and the hippocampus sense that the inputting sensory experience is dangerous or a threat, such as if the person is about to collide with an oncoming car, the experience is not processed in this normal way. Instead, the hypothalamus is activated and an immediate whole-body danger response is set off and a stress hormone is released. This causes connection with the pre-frontal cortex to shut down, blocking the experience from being given cognitive meaning. This process then triggers one, or more, of six primitive and subconscious survival mechanisms to deal with the danger.[5]

- *Fight.* The fight response kicks in when somebody feels a need to defend themselves from attack or threat. The fight response can manifest with aggressive and defensive anger, both verbally and physically.
- *Flight.* This is the instinct to run from danger. This can manifest as somebody withdrawing both socially or mentally as well as physically running. This might be seen in people avoiding certain situations or environments, suddenly ending relationships, or getting up and walking away quickly without any real explanation.
- *Freeze.* To stop all activities and to have the inability to move, like playing dead. This may manifest in a way that means a person can no longer function, they may not be able to move or speak and may have a blank, confused or dazed look on their face.
- *Fright.* This is when a person enters a state of high alert and hypervigilance. They are acutely aware of their surroundings and can notice subtle changes in the environment or people which others would not notice. The person is often attuned to the subtleties of body language and tone of voice of others around them. It causes panic attacks and severe anxiety, and makes people highly reactive to a perceived threat and unable easily to settle down.

- *Flop.* In its extreme state, this can be a total loss of body functions where the person faints, blacks out or has a seizure in response to perceived danger. However, in its less extreme form, the flop response can cause vomiting, unexplained physical pain, migraines, confusion or brain fog, a feeling of dissociation and disconnection, the loss of bladder and bowel functions, and sudden exhaustion.
- *Fawn.* The fawn response masks and hides the feelings of terror and fear when a person is in danger by putting the person into a submissive state by giving in, surrendering, becoming compliant, doing what they are told and avoiding conflict at all costs. This is usually a response to threat-filled environments which cannot be avoided or run from, such as domestic or family violence situations.[6]

These survival mechanisms are a form of protection which allow the brain to respond to danger automatically and subconsciously. For example, it is these survival mechanisms which force us automatically to pull our hand away when we touch a hot pan.

Suffering can be a painful process while one or more of these six survival responses is being triggered, but they are God-designed to allow the sufferer to survive, and therefore take over both the body and mind while the danger is still present. Once the danger has passed, the stress hormone stops releasing and the connection with the pre-frontal cortex is reactivated. The amygdala is then able to process the experience in the brain's normal way by moving the experience into the pre-frontal cortex, allowing meaning, language and rational processing to be given to the experience; the memory, although painful, is then able to be stored in the long-term memory. Therefore, every human will at some point have painful experiences stored in their long-term memory that may take many years fully to heal from. Some form of counselling or talking therapy may be required to help process and deal with those painful memories, but they are not trauma. The distinction between an experience of suffering and an experience of trauma is determined in the aftermath of the suffering being experienced.

A psychological trauma wound occurs when a person has reached their psychological pain threshold and they are taken beyond their window of tolerance. This means a person has experienced suffering which has been far too painful for them to endure. Or a person has experienced too many suffering experiences too frequently, particularly at a young age. This takes the survivor beyond the survival capabilities of the six survival mechanisms and the connection with the pre-frontal cortex remains shut down even once the danger has passed and the experience is therefore not able to be processed in the normal way.

The Trauma Brain

This inability eventually to process the suffering experience in the normal way has created a psychological trauma wound with profound biological and physical effects on the brain. Over time this causes the hippocampus and the pre-frontal cortex to shrink. The amygdala becomes overactive and connection with the pre-frontal cortex becomes decreased, fragmented and rewired. This means that the normal chain reaction function of the body and psychological processes has been overridden, and the suffering experienced was not given rational, cognitive meaning in the brain and was not moved and stored into the long-term memory. This means the suffering remains unregulated, felt and trapped in the short-term memory. Over time this causes a reliving of the experience; instead of survivors being able to call up or recount the memory at will, simple and seemingly unrelated experiences in the present can trigger the reliving process, meaning that for a trauma survivor, the present is repeatedly taken over by the past. This causes the experience to be constantly felt by the amygdala as an immediate and current danger experience, continually forcing connection with the pre-frontal cortex to shut down and one or more of the six survival mechanisms to be activated. In this way they are no longer simply survival mechanisms; they have become the brain's response to trauma.

To experience this continual cycle is to experience a fractioning and rewiring of the brain's normal functioning, causing a breakdown and disconnection of that which the survivor once knew to be certain and true in the world. While they are being affected by this rewiring the survivor may process and understand all new experiences and relationships from the perspective of being under threat. This profoundly affects the survivor because by processing new experiences as dangerous, the entire body system is constantly on high alert, potentially triggering one, if not more, of the six trauma responses in response to anything difficult, triggering or unfamiliar, even when there is no current danger or suffering. This often leads survivors to live chaotic and messy lifestyles where they exhibit any number of distressing behaviours such as eating disorders, self-harm, excessive anger, addiction and substance abuse, social isolation and withdrawal, low self-esteem, dissociation, numbing, fatigue and unexplained chronic medical problems, to name but a few. In this way, the brain's initial inbuilt protective design, originally intended to cope with suffering, has caused a psychological wound when a person is taken beyond their psychological window of tolerance with debilitating, long-lasting effects. Therefore, the wounding of trauma could be considered a form of brain injury rather than a mental illness.

The wounding of trauma could be considered a form of brain injury

It is important to be aware that this psychological window of tolerance is different for everyone, meaning the kind of suffering experience that may be considered trauma—to have created this psychological trauma wound—for one person may not be considered trauma for another person. Caution must therefore be advised for anyone, whether it be friends, family, pastoral workers, or the trauma survivor themselves when comparing trauma and suffering experiences with those of others.

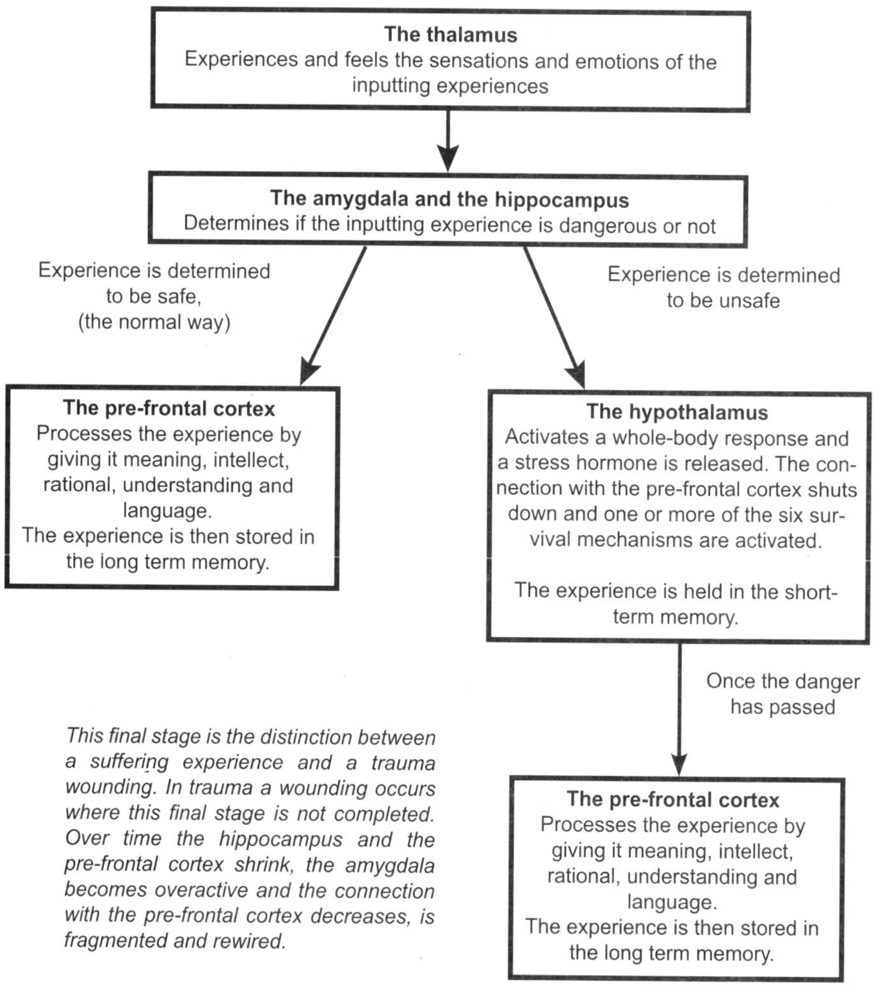

Figure 1: The process of how an experience is felt and processed by the brain.

3

Theology and Trauma

As human beings, our natural reaction is to try to remove ourselves from the issues of suffering and trauma. However, the Christian worshipping community cannot afford to do so because Jesus is not, and should not be, removed from these issues. Also, any Christian congregation today can reasonably be expected to include a significant number of trauma survivors who live with debilitating psychological trauma wounds. If the worshipping community is to meet the needs of all its members it must be prepared to ensure that its teachings, theology, doctrines and pastoral responses can speak to the lived experience of trauma survivors. To do this it is important to understand not only the physical or psychological wound of trauma, but that trauma is also a theological wounding. In trauma lies the fundamental question of the relationship between the good and loving creator of the universe and those who have survived suffering that has left them devastatingly wounded. This question may deeply impact survivors in many ways including a fear or rejection of God, church and any kind of religious belief, as well as a felt absence of God at a time when they needed him most. For those who know and trust in God's goodness and safety, this is a specific and unique pain and loss that is felt differently than by those who do not know God or trust in his goodness and safety.

Trauma is also a theological wounding

Those who have lived through indescribable suffering and whose memory, brain functions and identity have been distorted, rewired and fragmented by the psychological trauma wound are often forced to question if God does answer their cry for help, if he can be trusted, or even if he exists at all. In the aftermath of their trauma wound what remains for the survivor is an experience which revises what they once knew of the world before they experienced the suffering. If a person who has faith in God's ability to stop evil and hardship experiences trauma, their faith is often significantly challenged by the profound and painful realization that God did not stop the trauma from occurring. This is a sense of death in life, a theological death, where God as the giver of life is felt to be absent and distant from the lived experience of the Christian trauma survivor. For many Christians, redemption, salvation, forgiveness, freedom and wholeness are the go-to concepts when attempting to speak to the needs of healing for those who have survived trauma. In this narrative, a trauma survivor becomes a broken individual in need of fixing by something or somebody greater and more powerful than themselves. However, for survivors still living with psychological and theological trauma wounds, these themes could potentially be difficult and seemingly unattainable concepts. As we have seen the psychological trauma wound traps a survivor in a place in between trauma and healing, with a unique inability to feel fully alive. This is an experience where both what is in their past and what is in their future is unknown, painful and threatening. Survivors linger within an experience where they are not yet able fully to access the hope of the goodness and safety which the theology of redemption and salvation promises is yet to come. This is a problem which searches for some form of justice in the face of inconceivable injustice. For the Christian trauma survivor, therefore, the answer to their trauma pain cannot be solely secular but must also include a theological answer.

It is the cross of Jesus that is largely interpreted as the symbol of healing and salvation where it was God's plan for Jesus, his Son, to die so that he would win victory over death and in doing so humankind may be saved and redeemed to reconcile their sinful nature to God to gain eternal life. However, we cannot shy away from the reality that crucifixion was a horrific and torturous practice, and this horrific reality makes the crucifixion of Jesus a traumatic event. Yet Christianity widely continues to ask trauma survivors to look to the cross to find healing from the wounding that trauma has left them with. For many trauma survivors, this causes disturbing concerns, as they feel that to expect them as a survivor of trauma to find healing through an act of trauma is an unpalatable expectation, and potentially risks further traumatization.[7] Jesus' experience of suffering on the cross is often presented as good, loving and redemptive but in the face of trauma the question must be asked: how can redemptive torture be interpreted positively by a survivor of trauma as they recover from their own trauma experience? The fragmentation and rewiring of the brain in the psychological trauma wound creates an absence of any rational, psychologically integrated perception of new incoming experiences. This leaves very little possibility of a trauma survivor encountering and understanding the sacred in the same way as those who have not experienced trauma. Therefore, for pastoral care truly to be able to bring any kind of healing to trauma survivors it must allow the experience of trauma to inform and shape how healing is presented to a trauma survivor. Therefore, Jesus' experience of suffering on the cross should be told as a narrative of a struggle for justice in the aftermath of the trauma experience.

How can redemptive torture be interpreted positively by a survivor of trauma

The Traumatized God

As discussed, a trauma survivor cannot choose to set aside their trauma and is therefore forced to make their trauma an integral part of who they are while they remain trapped in a continuous cycle of reliving as well as the reactivation of the six trauma responses. This means the post-trauma experiences can often feel just as painful as the initial suffering experience itself and one of the most painful realities to contend with is that the past cannot be undone. The wound of trauma will always now in some way be a part of the survivor's story, even after any experience of healing and memory integration. If the theological wound of trauma is experienced as an absence of God, then arguably nothing less than the presence of God in the very raw, shattered and broken depths of the trauma wound can redeem and reconcile the wounded survivor to their creator. For any kind of healing of trauma to occur the wounding of trauma must be acknowledged by the worshipping community in a way that brings Jesus directly into the pain, and so this cannot be a simple acknowledgment. Pastoral care with trauma survivors must prioritize providing a way for them to connect with God's love and redemption in a way that acknowledges the depths of the trauma wounding and without asking them to do this by simply looking to an act of violence and trauma. To be able truly to do this we must present the cross of Jesus to trauma survivors in a way that is not potentially going to re-traumatize and does not focus on trauma being loving and redemptive.

Therefore, we must present the entire narrative of the passion of Jesus together as a whole rather than separating it into multiple narratives. For example, the willing submission of Jesus as seen in the Garden of Gethsemane must be told alongside the torture of the crucifixion, which in turn must be told alongside the death of Holy Saturday, which must be told alongside the resurrection of Easter Sunday. Christ could not rise from the dead if he did not die and without his resurrection, there is no divine act of healing or redemption. In the twentieth century, traditional interpretations of the crucifixion were revolutionized in this way by theologian Jurgen Moltmann, who asked the question, 'Where is God in the cross of the Christ who was abandoned by God?' Moltmann answered this question by arguing that God is found on the cross with Jesus, crucified with him as one.[8] Therefore, we can find that God is in the very depths of the trauma of Jesus on the cross; in the suffering of the trauma, the cross of Jesus is also the cross of the crucified God. If we present the passion in this way we will see the image of a traumatized God.

The traumatized God is an image in which God himself suffers with and for those who live with the wound of trauma, and through identification and solidarity he can directly relate to those who are survivors of trauma. During their trauma journey survivors can find comfort not only in the solidarity of the traumatized God on the cross but also in Jesus' actions following his resurrection, which here become a promise of something better out of pain. The post-trauma death experienced by survivors of the psychological and theological trauma wounds cannot be ignored or glossed over; rather, they need to become an integral part of the healing of trauma in the same way that the image of the traumatized God is to truly be an image of solidarity for trauma survivors. Understanding of the resurrected life of Jesus must also extend to the example set by his choice to resurrect with the physical wounds of his trauma intact. Had Christ wanted to distance himself from the atrocity of his suffering and trauma he arguably had the power and the ability to resurrect in perfect form without the crucifixion wounds. Instead, as seen in the holes left by the nails, he chose to confront trauma and the struggles of those who live with the wounding of trauma by placing himself in the very centre of the trauma experience. In the cross Jesus becomes a traumatized God; in the actions of Jesus following his resurrection, he becomes a trauma survivor.

In Luke 24.36–49, the resurrected Jesus appeared to his eleven disciples for the first time. As the disciples see him, they are afraid and question his identity by asking if he is a ghost. Jesus identifies himself to them by showing his hands and feet and their visible nail holes. In the showing of the nail holes, Jesus is placing great significance on them as the direct consequence and wounding of his trauma experience on the cross. This is an image in which even within the perfection of Jesus trauma has formed a lasting wound. Those who are survivors of trauma likewise live with the long-term debilitating wounds following their trauma experience. By using his trauma wounds to identify himself, the resurrected Jesus not only acknowledges his trauma, but invites his disciples to identify him through his trauma wounding. This is profound for trauma survivors because as Jesus chooses to reveal himself to his disciples allowing his trauma wounds to express silently his identity and allowing them to witness his trauma and the power of his resurrection Christian trauma survivors can see their trauma wounds as significant also. God chose to become a traumatized God on the cross and then to resurrect as a trauma survivor living with the wounds of trauma and using his trauma wounds to identify himself through which he promised hope to his disciples. This action not only meets the trauma survivor in their pain but as Emily Lyon describes, means that Jesus inhabits the broken souls of trauma survivors, 'suffering with them, struggling for life against all forces of evil which prey upon them' as he too struggled against all the forces of evil on the cross and then went on to own, live with and inhabit his trauma wounds which allowed his friends to witness his trauma and the power and testimony of God within in his post-trauma life.[9]

4

The Witnessing of Trauma

Talking therapy has for many years been the go-to within the NHS and the private healthcare sector when addressing the healing of psychological trauma as well as a wide variety of mental health issues. However, as we have seen, in complex trauma there are severe and lasting psychological consequences in which the sensational and emotional parts of the brain remain active but the meaning-making and cognitive part of the brain, the pre-frontal cortex, shrinks and is disconnected. This can render talking therapy useless in the healing of trauma. While survivors are still grappling with a lack of cognitive meaning, words—if they can be expressed at all—are insufficient to allow the survivor adequately to vocalize that they are experiencing pain, suffering and damage of a kind they are not yet psychologically able to comprehend or contextualize. The ability of trauma survivors to make any kind of quick or linear progression from the death of trauma to a life of healing is no longer known or available to them. Yet, as Manda explains, 'Paradoxically, it is precisely the confrontation of the suppressed trauma memory that is needed for inner healing.'[10] For trauma survivors unwilling or yet unable to attempt to engage directly verbally with their trauma experiences, they are left with a difficult and perilous crossroads in which it can sometimes seem from the survivor's perspective as though only harm will occur either way. Living well after trauma centres around the need for the trauma experience to be given meaning in the brain; this is done through the survivor telling the story of their trauma experiences, bringing the pain into the light, allowing the shame to lift and meeting Jesus in the very depths of their trauma wounds. Only by doing so can survivors who are deeply traumatized begin to feel safe and therefore be able to reconnect the pre-frontal cortex, allowing them to recover memories and give them meaning within the brain which they were never able to do at the time the experience occurred. However, survivors of complex trauma desire both to suppress their trauma and to talk about it, because to reactivate the pre-frontal cortex and eventually process the experience in the normal way requires the survivor to give the experience cognitive meaning, rationale and language, which forces them undergo a painful reliving process. To assign all trauma survivors with the expectation that they will be able to use talking therapy is therefore to

Living well after trauma centres around the trauma experience being given meaning

misunderstand the nature of the trauma experience entirely and is to expect survivors to complete a very painful, potentially harmful or even impossible task.

This misunderstanding can pose a great deal of risk, both to the survivor and to a pastoral caregiver. It is vitally important to accept that severely traumatized persons cannot immediately recount, communicate or give adequate meaning to their experiences. The shrinking and disconnection of the pre-frontal cortex often leads to a sensation of being trapped in silence because the pre-frontal cortex deals with intellect, communication and vocabulary. This is a silence in which any communication, even silent communication, with a trauma survivor is challenging. In some cases when the pre-frontal cortex is disconnected as an act of self-preservation, survivors can experience a type of forgetfulness and disconnection from the trauma experience which is called dissociation. Integrating or reconnecting these disconnected and dissociated memories is a long, difficult and often painful process that is sometimes never achieved for a survivor. It is for this reason that the primary goal for the pastoral caregiver should be to provide a safe and secure environment for the trauma survivor's healing to occur. As much as possible this initial process should seek continuously to affirm the trauma survivor, responding to them with dignity and encouraging and supporting the building of healthy relationships, forged through giving survivors autonomy and choice over their own healing narrative. It would be hard for anyone to trust somebody they have just met with their innermost untold story, let alone after that trust in others has already been shattered by any form of interpersonal trauma.

Pain has a voice which can communicate the depths of despair and cries for love

Recent studies in the areas of trauma care and trauma theology have attempted to address the concerns and issues surrounding the argued inadequacy of talking therapies. Research shows that more and more therapists are moving towards somatic therapy, 'a method that places the body at the centre of trauma care rather than focusing on conversation about trauma.'[11] This method of therapy focuses on how a person's feelings affect their physical body. It is a non-verbal form of therapy in which bodily symptoms are listened to. Pain has a voice, and it is that voice which can communicate the depths of despair and cries for love and belonging in the aftermath of trauma. Without the ability adequately to communicate the trauma pain verbally, or to be able independently to assign traumatic events context themselves, survivors can experience a crisis in their own identity, physical body and sense of self. Through somatic therapies involving activities such as deep breathing, dance, grounding techniques, hugs and massages, a survivor might be able to communicate their pain and be heard non-verbally by the pastoral caregiver who witnesses what their body is experiencing.

Traditionally theology and our worshipping communities have been far less informed about the effects of trauma on survivors than is needed to provide appropriate care. Arguably it is vital for anyone attempting to support trauma survivors in their healing to be informed and appropriately equipped to provide the deeply sensitive care needed. Considering the extremely challenging nature of caring for and ministering to trauma survivors from a Christian perspective, spiritual pastoral care needs to approach the healing of trauma differently than talking therapies do. Deusen Hunsinger describes pastoral care as 'first and foremost a theology of God's care for the world in Jesus Christ, in which we are invited to participate.'[12] If this is correct then arguably the practical outworking of pastoral theology is found in participation with the trauma pain and not in sitting at a distance and listening to a conversation about trauma. A relationship with Jesus is the complete and ultimate reparative relationship, and so any healing needs to come from a relationship with Jesus. The pastoral caregiver must not only participate in the trauma survivors' silent telling of their trauma narrative and witness their pain but must allow their participation in this witnessing to be in Jesus Christ. This suggests that it may be time to consider that the focus of pastoral care should not be about the healing, restoring or fixing of the trauma wounding, but should be about being in Jesus and witnessing the wounds of trauma.

Any healing needs to come from a relationship with Jesus

A crucial component of a trauma survivor beginning to heal is witnessing. This witnessing is not just listening to what is said but rather it is witnessing the brokenness and the unsayable; it is in this place that a trauma survivor can begin to find hope. In theological terms, silent witnessing is best presented to us in the Old Testament Book of Job, which provides a story of suffering and trauma and brings the horror of human suffering into the context of faith in a good God. When we read of the aftermath of Job's trauma we find a detailed insight into the role of reparative, witnessing relationships. Following Job's suffering his friends come to comfort him in his post-traumatic state. Their initial response in the face of his brokenness and trauma death is profound and significant: '…they sat with him on the ground for seven days and seven nights, and no one spoke a word to him, for they saw that his suffering was very great' (Job 2.12–13). This biblical passage confronts us with the healing found in silence. Here we see the sudden, shocking and painful reality of trauma wounds that have no words, and we are provided with a direct and literal description of witnessing. This kind of silence is not an emptiness or a nothingness, it is the consequence of the magnitude and gravity of the trauma pain and wounding. The silence of Job's friends was helpful and supportive, although the advice they went on to give was mistaken and disapproved of by God. This demonstration of witnessing, combined with the trauma narrative of Jesus, may enable our worshipping communities to begin to offer pastoral care in a way that offers true comfort to survivors. Like Job's friends who sit in the silence of the unsayable, like Jesus who entered the unsayable of the post-traumatic by experiencing the deadly outcome of his trauma in Holy Saturday and becoming a trauma survivor in his post-trauma resurrection, this is a call for our worshipping communities in this way to witness the suffering felt by survivors of trauma.

Building a Trauma-informed Worshipping Community

5

To be able to witness to the trauma pain of its members the worshipping community must first acknowledge that the wounding of trauma has taken the survivor beyond the realm of normal mental functioning. This creates deep feelings of powerlessness, isolation and hopelessness. Both the survivor's ability to see themselves as a creation of God and their ability to connect spiritually with God and his people has been impaired. This makes it difficult for a trauma survivor to connect meaningfully to others within any community, especially a community which attempts to communicate themes of hope, healing and life. The apostle Paul says that it is through Jesus that all things hold together and that through Jesus, God is reconciling to himself everything and everyone (Col 1.17–20). As we have explored, liberation, healing and safety can only be comprehended for a trauma survivor if their suffering is first acknowledged in a way that makes Jesus present in the acknowledgment. Therefore, the hope found in Jesus and the healing of the trauma wounds is a form of liberation in which Jesus himself becomes the liberating presence when he became a trauma survivor himself, standing in solidarity with those who are survivors of trauma.

The whole worshipping community must dare to face, acknowledge, witness and embody the suffering of all those within their community, allowing the wounds of trauma to shape and inform the ethos, culture, practices and traditions of the community. This must be a truly active and deliberate involvement where the community allows the lived experience of the trauma wound to inform and shape who they are.

What Does this Mean Practically for the Worshipping Community?

Due to the complex and deeply personal nature of trauma, it is never easy to offer clear practical suggestions on how a worshipping community would build a trauma-informed community. Equally, it would never be possible to provide an extensive list of practical applications in this booklet. However, in this final chapter, this booklet seeks to offer some practical suggestions which could support worshipping communities in beginning to become trauma-informed and therefore better able to support its members who are survivors of psychological trauma.

Training and Knowledge

Survivors who choose to turn to pastoral care for guidance in their recovery and rehabilitation are often met with theological practitioners unaccustomed to the unique care they require. Already it is clear that within the worshipping community, the preacher ought always to preach as if a survivor of the most horrific trauma were present, considering their words and how they communicate the presence of Jesus in the word. Likewise, our pastoral care must consider the needs of those deeply wounded by the psychological trauma wound. Only through understanding trauma and its effects on the brain and the way a survivor behaves and processes all new experiences can somebody truly be able to walk alongside those who live with it. Hope, belonging and flourishing can only occur when the trauma survivor feels understood and noticed in their pain and despite their pain. This can only happen through the worshipping community normalizing living alongside those who live with psychological trauma wounds. This must be done by talking about trauma, teaching, providing training and equipping all within the community, especially those working to support survivors, with accurate knowledge and understanding of how the psychological wounding of trauma has occurred and impacted the everyday mental functioning and behaviours of those within the community they are walking alongside. Through a deeper understanding of the psychological trauma wound and how the six trauma responses trap a survivor in their past and impact their behaviours in the present, it will then become possible to hear the cry of trauma and to witness the shattering of the soul in a way that brings Jesus into the very depths of the trauma pain.

Relate to the Limbic System

It is important to consider what the psychological trauma wound and the continual subconscious activation of one or more of the six trauma responses might mean for a survivor's behaviours, actions and responses. It is important for the pastoral caregiver to respond in an understanding, non-judgmental and compassionate way while also gently challenging inappropriate behavioural responses. Consider how it must feel constantly to experience all new experiences as though being under threat. Consider your tone of voice, volume and body language. Create a connection which allows you to speak love and the restoration of Jesus rather than offering reproach. Model and show the love that Jesus has for survivors. Listen to their wounds and allow their pain to be witnessed by you.

Develop Good Boundaries

Trauma is complex and due to the nature of the psychological trauma wound the life of a survivor can be chaotic, unpredictable and messy. It is never appropriate, and can even be dangerous, for those in the worshipping community who are not qualified professionals to work with survivors of trauma in recovering and reintegrating trauma memories. It is the survivor's responsibility to work with Jesus, alongside trained professionals, to find their own healing and liberation. A worshipping community cannot do more for somebody than they are willing to do for themselves. However, it is the worshipping community's role to provide a place of safety and belonging by walking alongside and deeply witnessing the struggle of trauma. To do this appropriately, clear and consistent boundaries must be in place. It is important to be clear from the start of any relationship with a survivor of trauma what you can and cannot offer and what is your role in their life. Explain to the survivor how much time you can give them and be clear and consistent with what you can give and the ways they can contact you. Comments like 'Give me a call any time you need' or 'I am always here for you' might feel to us to be caring and supportive but they are not realistic and are promises that cannot be kept. The chaotic and messy lifestyle of someone living with psychological trauma wounds often means they are not able to regulate appropriate social boundaries. Therefore, it is the role of the pastoral caregiver and the worshipping community to be clear in setting appropriate boundaries and expectations for the relationship. This is imperative for the safety and health of all within the community, including the pastoral caregiver as well as the survivor of trauma.

It is the worshipping community's role to provide a place of safety and belonging

Give Choice and Autonomy

Walking alongside a survivor and witnessing their trauma is not about doing something to the survivor or for the survivor. Likewise, it cannot be about fixing the survivor, especially as it takes many years for the psychological trauma wound to heal and there is rarely, if ever, a complete healing 'fix.' Allow yourself to ask the individual trauma survivors in your community what they need to feel safety and belonging within your worshipping community. Witness their pain, walk alongside them, and allow their voice, non-verbal story, and psychological trauma responses to inform your worshipping community's teachings, doctrines and pastoral practices. Together you will struggle to find justice in the face of injustice, caring for one another, loving one another and building a community where all have a chance to flourish. It has often been an unfortunate reality that the voice, feelings and choices of survivors themselves have not been listened to in the way that our worshipping communities have attempted to support trauma survivors in the past. It is also a painful reality that choice and agency have often been stolen from the survivor in some way during their suffering experience and so restoring agency and choice to a survivor is vital. Ask the survivor what they need and allow them to express how they would like to be supported. Remember trauma does not sit in the language part of the brain, so it is important to listen to what the survivor is expressing through their behaviours and actions not just what they are saying with their words.

Giving autonomy, agency and choice also means allowing the survivor to make their own choices which they are responsible for, including choosing to make harmful choices. Part of being a safe, trauma-informed community must be about giving everyone the freedom of choice, even if we do not like or agree with the choices they make. Walking alongside the survivor and witnessing their trauma then becomes about giving safe unconditional love as Jesus would. Allowing the survivor the freedom to make these choices even if we do not agree with them does not mean there are no consequences to the choices made. It may be there are times when it is appropriate for a church leader, friend or pastoral caregiver who has developed a trusting relationship with the survivor to challenge unacceptable behaviours, even if their reasons are understood, and to support and challenge the survivor in responding to perceived unsafe situations differently in the future.

Consider How Changes Affect Trauma Survivors

For survivors of trauma changes to the normal routine or the environment can often feel unsafe and threatening. Therefore, consistency and stability can support a survivor to feel safer. This does not mean a worshipping community should never do anything new or make any changes. However, implementing simple but effective trauma-informed practices such as providing a warning that changes are happening would support a survivor in feeling safer despite the changes. Discussing the changes with the survivor beforehand and providing the survivor with some suggestions such as someone they feel safe with, such as a pastoral caregiver, could sit with them, at least initially, or asking the survivor what they need to feel safe will support the survivor to make an informed choice, and to consider how they will respond to the changes and to prepare for them. This means that when the changes have been made it is less likely to trigger one or more of the six trauma responses.

Consider the Physical Environment

When building a trauma-informed worshipping community it is also important to consider the physical environment in which the community might meet. The need for a survivor to feel physically safe in an environment is as equally vital for the building of trauma-informed communities as it is for a survivor to feel emotionally safe. One example is that for many survivors having the agency to choose where they sit during a service or meeting rather than being told is vital to feeling safe. Likewise, having clear, unblocked access to the exits. For example, not having someone sit in front of a doorway during a meeting or Bible study group supports the survivor with not feeling trapped, and feeling like they could get out if they needed to, even if this is never needed.

Equally, many worship services, particularly if crowded and busy, can often feel overstimulating for a trauma survivor whose experiences are continually processed by the brain as unsafe or threatening and therefore triggering one or more of the six trauma responses. An example of how to alleviate this might be to ensure there are quieter parts of the room, such as at the back away from people, or even a separate breakout room which survivors of trauma have the freedom to access when needed to help them feel safe.

Consider How Our Actions May Re-traumatize

We need to be aware that the things we say and do have the potential to re-traumatize survivors of trauma who are living with psychological trauma wounds. While we can never be certain we will never re-traumatize or trigger one of the six trauma responses, we must provide trauma-informed communities that aim to be safe and supportive for all. This means it is important to consider how our words and actions may affect others. For example, be mindful of the way we show care and welcoming through physical contact such as hugs and a reassuring hand on the arm as these can heighten memories of past experiences where touch was not safe. Therefore always check it is ok to touch a trauma survivor. Also by providing trigger warnings we can support survivors of trauma who might be affected or feel unsafe by certain topics of discussion, particularly during a sermon. Offering a warning about the upcoming topic allows the trauma survivor the choice to leave the room if the topic is going to be too traumatizing or triggering for them. It also allows them time to process the upcoming topic and so when it is mentioned it does not hold the same impact and feelings of unsafety which would activate one or more of the six trauma responses.

Conclusion

It is Jesus who calls us to be safe, trauma-informed worshipping communities, and it is only with Jesus and through Jesus that we can support survivors of trauma. As mentioned, nothing less than the real presence of Jesus in the depths of the trauma pain can truly reconcile the wounded survivor to God. Pastoral care is us participating in God's care in the world through Jesus; this means that we cannot build a trauma-informed worshipping community without the presence of Jesus. We are therefore called to love one another, walk alongside one another and genuinely be committed to each other's good. As we love one another, sit with each other in the pain and witness the horror of their trauma we will allow the trauma survivor themselves the opportunity to meet with Jesus in the depths of their trauma pain to find the healing and safety they have come to our worshipping community to seek.

To build a trauma-informed worshipping community is to build a community where all are involved and none are left out. Where survivors belong and feel safe despite their trauma wounds. Jonathan Bradford says this would be to build a 'state of wholeness, harmony, delight, and balance where all people have an equal chance to flourish and to use their God-given gifts without impediment.'[13] In the gospels we see Jesus' example of what this community would look like through the image of his disciples and followers living, worshipping and ministering together, encouraging one another, and not neglecting meeting together. As Peter Dibley says, meeting together is 'to care for one another, to love one another and to do good deeds because we are, as Scripture asserts, better together.'[14] This type of community is deeper than a physical act of being together but is also an inward state of togetherness which allows a space where those who suffer can be seen, acknowledged, witnessed, accepted and belong.

As we have seen, healing begins for those living with trauma when those around them dare to look into the face of their suffering and walk alongside them by witnessing and embodying the pain of trauma, allowing it to shape and inform the practices of the community. Only then can the worshipping community truly be a trauma-informed community where all have a genuine commitment to each other's good and only then do all have the chance to flourish. To have someone walk alongside you and to witness the unspeakable and indescribable wounding found in the aftermath of trauma is a deeply profound act of compassion for a trauma survivor. To have a person sit with a trauma survivor in the depths of their brokenness, to see them and to know them, to witness the atrocity of their pain and the wounds it has left them with, is an image of belonging and of the pastoral caregiver participating in God's care in the world through Jesus. To provide this deep sense of belonging and witness to a trauma survivor is what it is to be a trauma-informed worshipping community where those who have experienced what it is to survive insurmountable pain find Jesus in the depths of their pain also.

Notes

1 C Manda, 'Re-authoring life narratives of trauma survivors: Spiritual Perspective' in *Theological Studies* 71(2), 2015, p 2.

2 J E Beste, *God and the Victim: Traumatic Intrusions on Grace and Freedom* (Oxford University Press, 2008) p 5.

3 S Rambo, 'Introduction' in S N Arel and S Rambo (eds), *Post-traumatic Public Theology* (New York: Palgrave Macmillan, 2016) p 3.

4 See B Van Der Kolk, *The Body Keeps the Score: Mind, Brain and Body in the Transformation of Trauma* (London: Penguin Random House, 2014).

5 B Van Der Kolk, *op cit.*

6 R Harris, *Trauma-Focused Act: A Practitioner's Guide to Working with Mind, Body, and Emotion Using Acceptance and Commitment Therapy* (New Harbinger Publications, 2021).

7 J Jobling, 'Post-Christian Hermeneutics' in L Isherwood and K McPhillips (ed), *Post-Christian Feminism: A Critical Approach* (Hampshire: Ashgate Publishing Limited, 2008).

8 J Moltmann, *The Crucified God: The Cross of Christ as the Foundation and Criticism of Christian Theology* (New York: Harper and Row, 1973).

9 E Lyon, 'The Spiritual Implications of Interpersonal Abuse: Speaking of the Soul,' *Pastoral Psychology 59*, 2010, p 245.

10 C Manda, 'Re-authoring life narratives of trauma survivors: Spiritual Perspective' in *Theological Studies* 71(2), 2015, p 2.

11 P Browning Helsel, 'Witnessing the Body's Response to Trauma: Resistance, Ritual, and Nervous System Activation,' in *Pastoral Psychology 64,* 2015, p 683.

12 D Van Deusen Hunsinger, 'Bearing the Unbearable; Trauma, Gospel and Pastoral Care' in *Theology Today,* 2011, p 9.

13 J Bradford, 'Building Shalom Communities: The Bricks and Boards, Dollars and Cents of Housing Justice,' in *Social Work and Christianity 33,* 2006, p 392.

14 P Dibley, 'Do not forsake the assembly: The importance of Christian community,' in *Review and Expositor* 115, 2018, p 408.